I0817003

DREAM JOBS If You Like ROBOTS

by Amie Jane Leavitt

CAPSTONE PRESS
a capstone imprint

Capstone Captivate is published by Capstone Press, an imprint of Capstone.
1710 Roe Crest Drive
North Mankato, Minnesota 56003
www.capstonepub.com

Library of Congress Cataloging-in-Publication Data is available on the Library of Congress website.
ISBN: 978-1-4966-8397-7 (library binding)
ISBN: 978-1-4966-8448-6 (eBook PDF)

Summary: Wouldn't it be cool to have a job working with or around the things you love? Do you have an interest in artificial intelligence? Maybe working with robots would compute for you! Readers will discover the possibilities of careers working with robots.

Image Credits
Alamy: FORGET Patrick, 21; Getty Images: Onfokus, 29; NASA, 26; National Institute of Standards and Technology, 13; Newscom: Yonhap News/YNA, 24; Shutterstock: ArtHead, (circuit pattern) Cover, BigBlueStudio, 9, Elliott Cowand Jr, 28, Flashon Studio, 20, Fotokostic, 7, Gorodenkoff, back cover, 4, guruXOX, 10, Jenson, 8, MIKHAIL GRACHIKOV, (dots) Cover, Monstar Studio, 19, Photomontage, 12, Prasert Sripodok, 11, Sundry Photography, 23, Suwin, 18, Tatyaby, (robot) Cover, Tyler Olson, 15, zaferkizilkaya, 17

Editorial Credits
Editor: Heather Williams; Designer: Sara Radka; Media Researcher: Morgan Walters; Production Specialist: Spencer Rosio

All internet sites appearing in back matter were available and accurate when this book was sent to press.

Printed in the United States
PA117

Table of Contents

Words in **bold** are in the glossary.

There are millions of jobs in the world. But only a few are dream jobs. A dream job might not make you rich, but you will love going to work every day. If you love playing with robots, watching them in movies, or programming them, one of these could end up being your dream job.

Robotics Engineer

Robot vacuums clean our houses. Giant robots make our cars. Rolling robots deliver food and packages. Some robots even teach school! Who builds the bodies for these robots? That is the job of a robotics engineer.

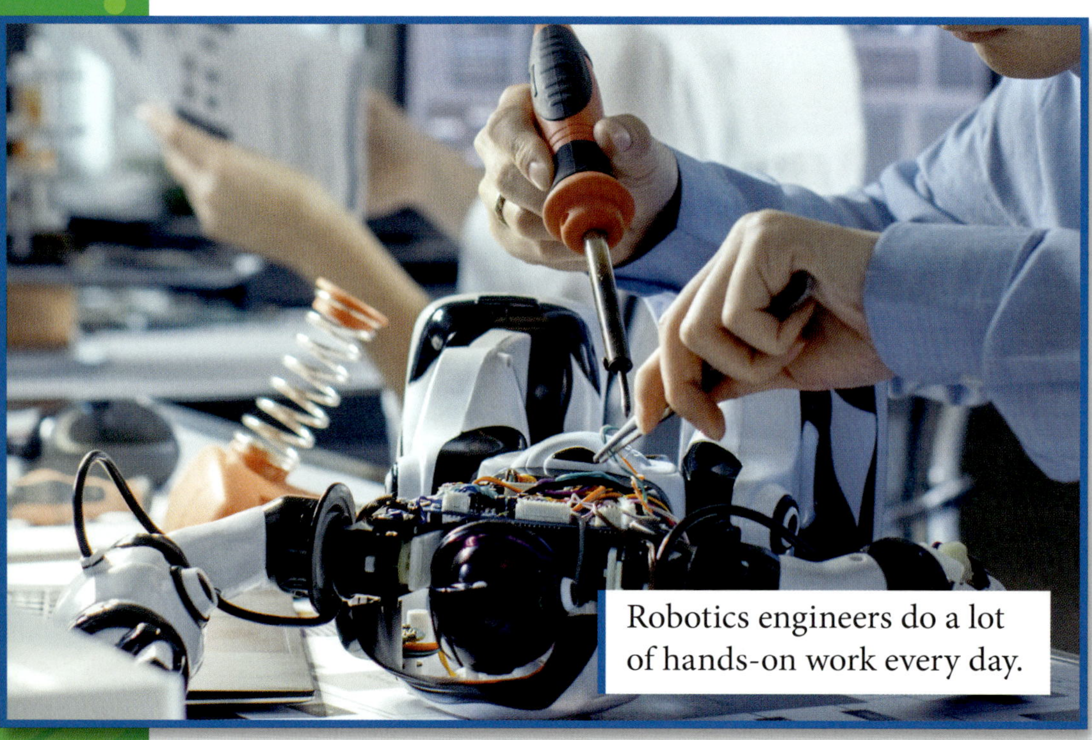

Robotics engineers do a lot of hands-on work every day.

On the Job

Robotics engineers first decide what jobs their robot will do. Then they draw the plans for the robot. Robots have moving parts. They roll on wheels. They move their arms to lift and carry things. These movements let them do different jobs. Next the engineers choose building materials, such as plastic or metal. Finally, the engineers build a **prototype**. They give the robot body to a software engineer. That person builds the robot's brain. The brain makes the robot move.

FUN FACT

Robots can work in extreme places such as volcanoes, on the ocean floor, and on the surface of other planets.

Pay Range

Average salary = $97,000 per year.

Education and Skills

Robotics engineers go to college. They go for four or more years. They study engineering and robotics. They also study how machines are built. Many robotics engineers are good with math and science. They also enjoy building things that have moving parts. They like knowing how things work. Engineers enjoy solving puzzles. They have to be willing to try many solutions before they find the right answer.

21st-Century Farmer

Most people know that food comes from farms. But did you know that many farmers use robots to help them grow this food? These robots help them do their work faster. Farming robots do jobs that require a lot of labor. This lets the farmer focus on more important tasks.

On the Job

Robots help farmers in many ways. Some robots pull weeds. Others check the soil to see if crops need water. Robots may help pick fruit and vegetables. They may round up cattle and bring them home from the range. Not all farmers use robots. But experts think more and more farmers will be using them in the future.

Pay Range

Salary varies for farmers. **Commercial** farmers often make more than those who run small family farms. The average is $75,000 per year, but it can also be much less than that.

Education and Skills

Farmers often work from sunrise to sunset. They spend most of their time outdoors. They work with plants and animals. Farmers use many different types of tools and machinery to do their jobs.

FUN FACT

The SwagBot is a robot dog used in Australia. It helps ranchers round up, feed, and keep track of their livestock.

Machines such as combine harvesters make gathering crops faster and easier.

Robots make car manufacturing faster and safer.

Manufacturer

What do cars, toys, and exercise equipment have in common? Many were made in factories with the help of robots.

On the Job

People who work in factories are called manufacturers. They make things to sell. Many factories have robot workers too. Some robots do jobs that are too dangerous for humans. Others work with human workers. They help them get jobs done faster.

Pay Range

Average salary = $48,000 per year.

FUN FACT

A cobot is a robot that is meant to work alongside humans. *Cobot* is short for "collaborative robot."

Education and Skills

People who work in manufacturing must like to work with tools. They often use tools to put things together. They must also like to do the same things over and over again. Many manufacturing jobs are on an **assembly line**. Every person on the assembly line has one task to do. They repeat this task on every item that is built.

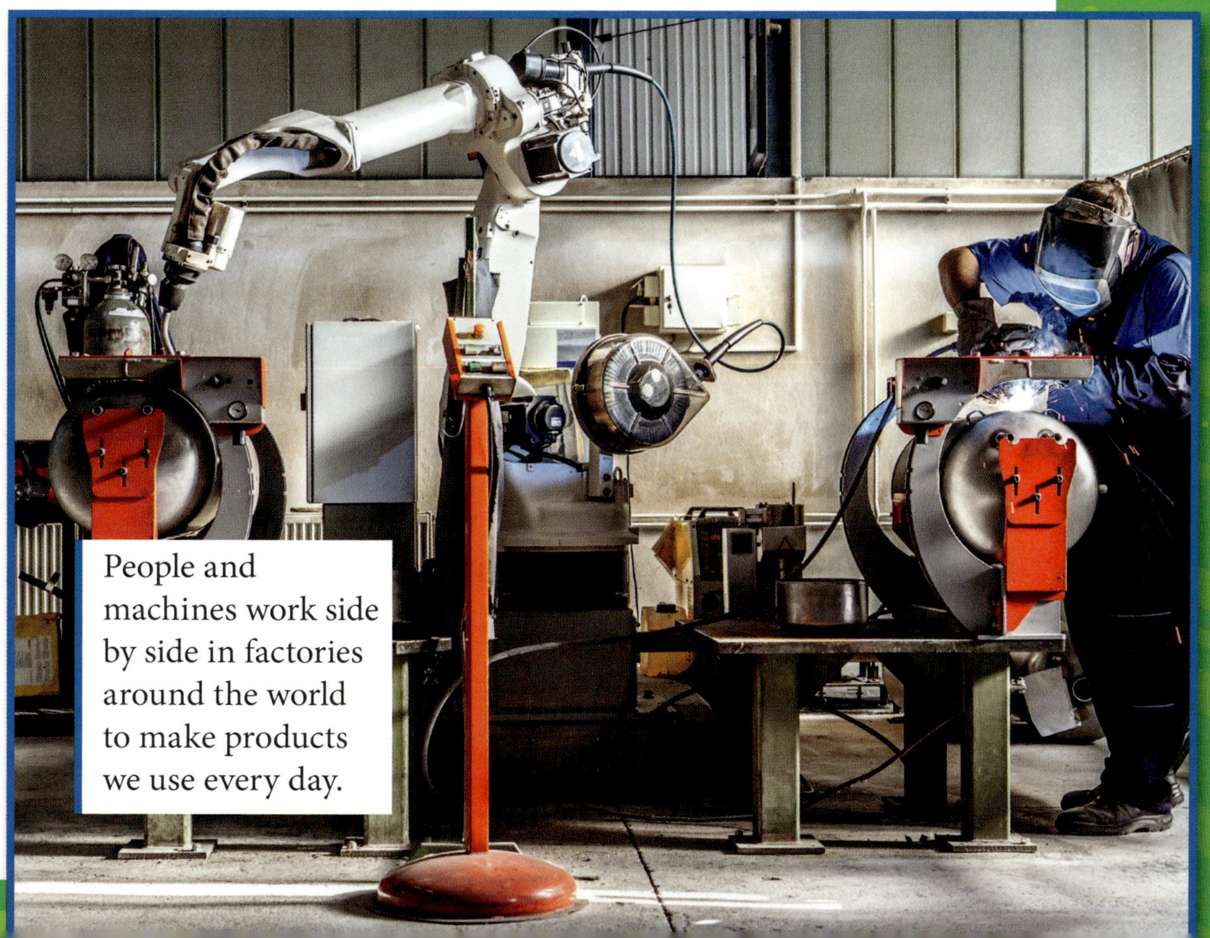

People and machines work side by side in factories around the world to make products we use every day.

Filmmakers need a good understanding of technology, including special cameras, lights, and even robots.

Filmmaker

Filmmakers often work with robots. Robots have jobs behind the scenes. Robotic **drones** help film **aerial** views from high above a scene. Someday robots might even be cast as actors.

On the Job

Many filmmakers work in studios. There are many film studios in Hollywood. They also work on location. This means they make movies in places around the world. They make movies for entertainment. Filmmakers also make **documentaries** about certain topics. Filmmakers direct actors. They work with modern technology such as cameras, computers, and drones. They often work long hours every day until filming is finished.

Pay Range

Salary varies greatly and can range from $73,000 to $95,000 per year.

Education and Skills

Many filmmakers go to college. They study film or photography. Some learn by working with other filmmakers. They must know how to use filmmaking equipment. They must also know how to read **scripts** and direct actors.

FUN FACT

Stuntronics are robots that do stunts in movies. These robots twirl and spin like human acrobats. They also do things that may be too dangerous for human stunt actors to do.

Drone cameras allow filmmakers to easily capture sporting events and other action-packed moments.

Rescuer

Sometimes people need to be rescued. They might get buried under snow while skiing. They could get trapped under rocks in an earthquake. Luckily, search and rescue people come to help. They often bring robots with them to do the job.

On the Job

Search and rescue people help at disasters. Their job is to find people who are trapped. Some places are too dangerous for rescuers to enter. Robot rescuers are called to the scene. They can swim and fly. They can crawl through the rubble of a fallen building. Rescue robots are built with cameras and microphones. These send information back to the rescuers. When the robot finds a person, the rescuers and robots work together to get that person out safely.

Special fire-fighting robots can put out fires so rescue workers can search for people.

Pay Range

Some rescuers work as volunteers. Others earn an average salary of between $34,000 and $45,000 per year.

Education and Skills

Search and rescue people like to help others. Most are trained in CPR and first aid. They also get trained in certain types of rescue. Some focus on mountain and cave rescue. Some are experts in **urban** building rescue. Others are experts in ocean rescue. They must know how to use many different types of tools and equipment for their jobs. They use compasses, maps, computers, and robots.

FUN FACT

Some rescue robots can hear a heartbeat from 30 feet (9 meters) away. They can tell if the heartbeat is a person or animal. This information tells rescuers if someone is trapped in a building, even if that person cannot cry out.

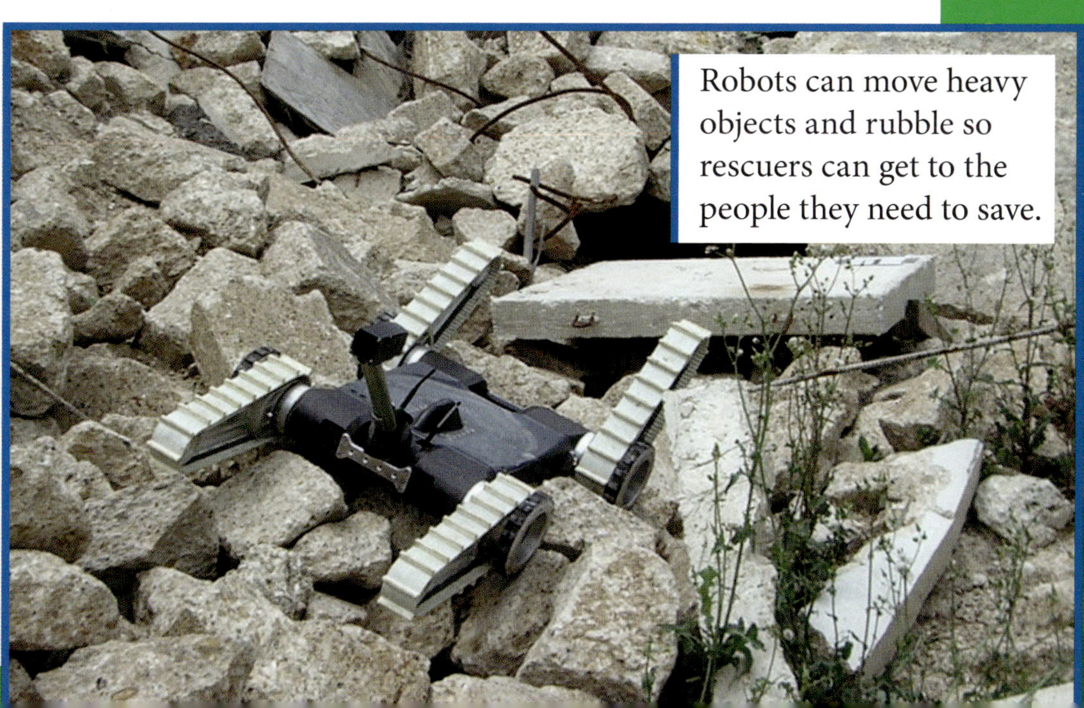

Robots can move heavy objects and rubble so rescuers can get to the people they need to save.

Health-Care Worker

Many people work in the health-care field. Doctors and nurses take care of people who are sick. Technicians take X-rays and other images. Surgeons correct problems inside a person's body. All health-care workers use modern technology. Some use robots to help them do their jobs better.

On the Job

The main job of health-care workers is helping people stay healthy. Robots give these workers an extra helping hand. They assist surgeons in delicate surgeries. They aid doctors in spotting diseases. Robots helped with more than 750,000 surgeries worldwide in 2016. The health-care field is expected to use robots even more in the future.

Pay Range

Salary varies, depending upon the job. Per year, it can range from $38,000 for technicians to $500,000 for surgeons.

Education and Skills

College is required for most health-care jobs. Health-care workers study how the human body works. They learn about ways to care for patients. They learn how to use technology such as computers, medical tools, and even robots. Most work long shifts of 12 hours or more. People in this field must be able to work well with little sleep.

FUN FACT

Some patients have been asked to swallow pill-size robots. The bots travel through the patient's **digestive system**. They send back pictures for the doctor to review. This is a new technology that may be used more in the future.

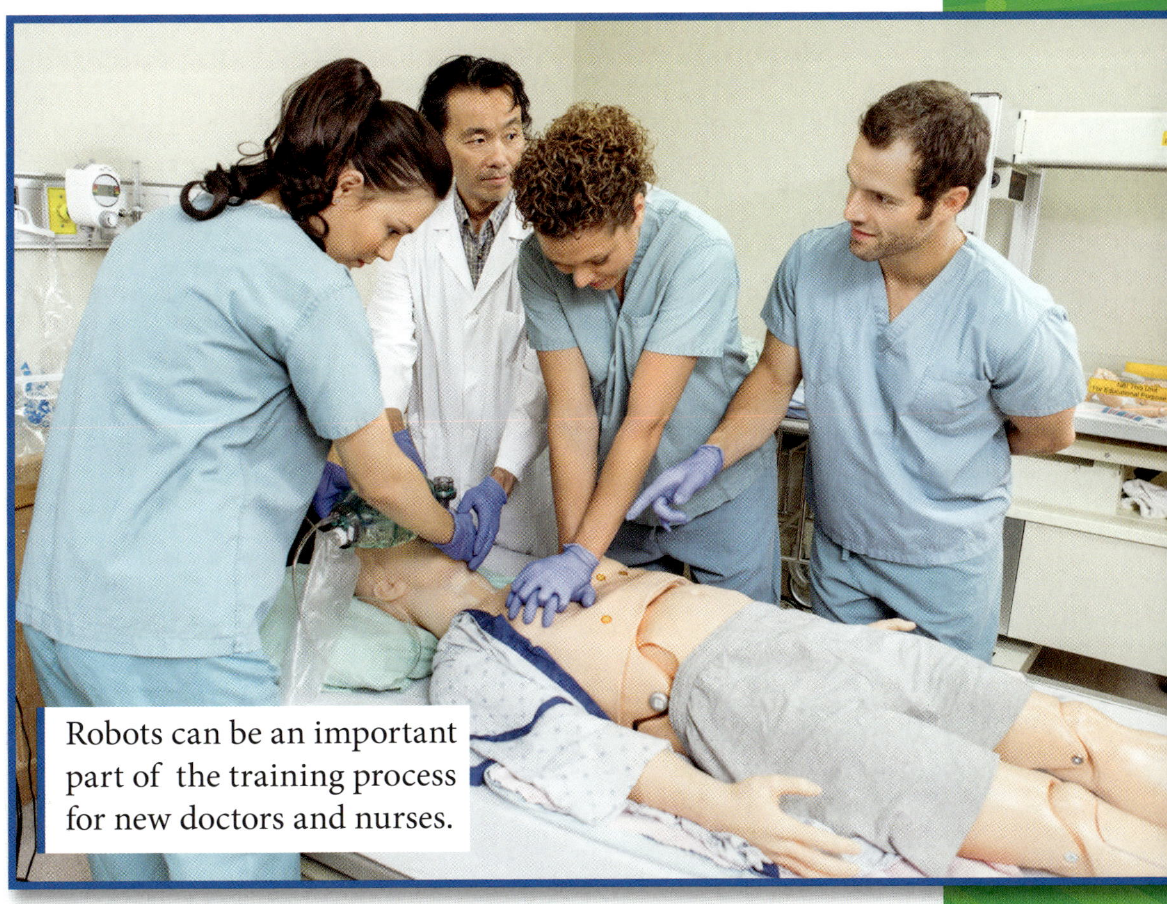

Robots can be an important part of the training process for new doctors and nurses.

Marine Scientist

Marine scientists study the world's oceans and ocean floors. Oceans cover most of Earth's surface. Yet less than 20 percent of the ocean floors have been mapped. That is because most of them are too deep for humans to reach. The Mariana Trench is the deepest part of the ocean floor. It is deeper than Mount Everest is high! Marine scientists need special robotic vehicles to study such areas.

On the Job

Marine scientists spend a lot of time on or near the water. They send **autonomous** underwater vehicles (AUVs) into the ocean. AUVs have built-in cameras. They take pictures of the ocean floor. They photograph the plants and animals that live there. Scientists would have difficulty getting this information without these robots.

Pay Range

Average salary = $50,000 per year.

Marine scientists use a variety of technology to study life underwater.

Education and Skills

Most marine scientists go to college for more than four years. They study biology, zoology, and geology. They are able to work with technology like computers and robots. Marine scientists are also team players. They work with others to gather and study the data they find.

FUN FACT

The *Scarlet Knight* is an AUV. It was the first robotic vehicle to travel across an ocean. It traveled from New Jersey to Spain in 2009.

Software Engineer

Software engineers make computer programs. They make "brains" for robots! They program robots to do many different types of tasks.

On the Job

Software engineers spend much of their time in front of a computer screen. They know many computer programming languages. These include languages such as Python, Lua, Java, and C++. Software engineers write programs in these computer languages. The programs include special instructions called code. Code tells the robot what tasks to do.

A robot might be programmed to perform a short series of steps, or it might be able to do several different tasks.

Pay Range

Average salary = $78,000 per year.

Education and Skills

Most software engineers have a college degree. They study computer science. They are good at math and science. Software engineers often start out by learning computer languages. They take classes in computer coding so they can write programs.

FUN FACT

FIRST LEGO League holds a robotics competition for kids in kindergarten through 8th grade. More than 35,140 teams from around the world participated between 2018 and 2019.

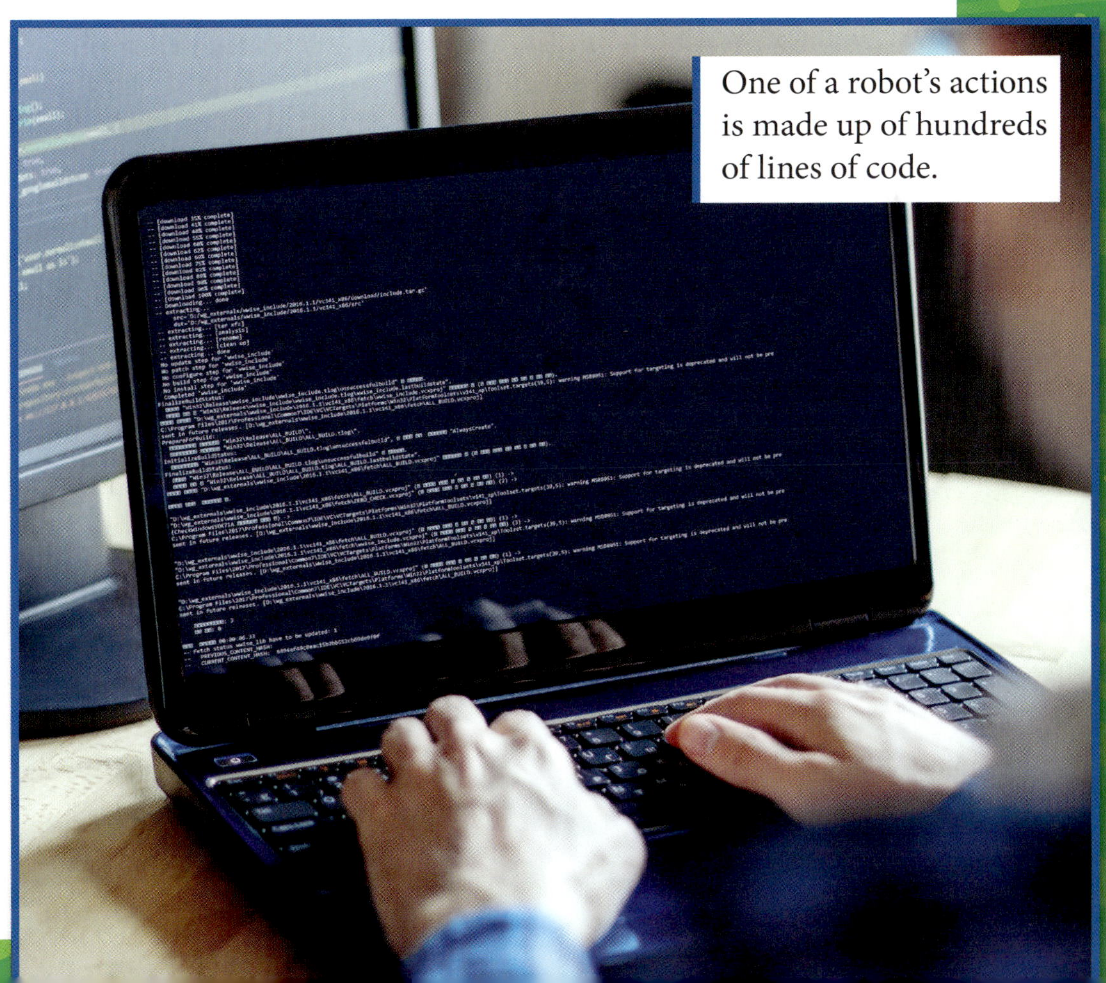

One of a robot's actions is made up of hundreds of lines of code.

Firefighter

Firefighters put out fires. They are brave people. Their jobs are very dangerous. Firefighters don't have to fight alone in today's world. Many use robots to help them stay safe in the line of duty.

On the Job

Fires can happen at any time and in almost any place. Firefighters must be able to carry and use different kinds of equipment for different kinds of fires. Robots can help firefighters in many ways. Some robots are remote-controlled vehicles. The firefighters can send these robots into a blaze. The robots can reach areas where human firefighters cannot safely go. Firefighters also use drones to put out fires from the air. Robot firefighters are used to put out forest wildfires and fires on ships at sea.

Pay Range

Average salary = $45,000 per year.

Education and Skills

Many firefighters earn a certificate in fire science. Firefighters must be strong and able to carry heavy equipment. They must be physically fit. Firefighters also need to know how to use machines and technology such as robots and drones. They need to be able to stay calm. They need to have good judgment skills to know how to handle an emergency. Firefighters must be trained and certified in first aid and CPR too.

FUN FACT

When the Notre Dame Cathedral in Paris, France, caught fire in 2019, a robot firefighter named Colossus helped put out the blaze. Colossus is waterproof and fire-resistant. It can spray 660 gallons (2,498 liters) of water per minute. Firefighters can control Colossus from 1,000 feet (305 m) away.

Robotic firefighters can get closer to fires than humans can, so they make putting out a fire safer and faster.

Driverless Vehicle Engineer

A self-driving auto is a vehicle that drives without a human in the driver's seat. Self-driving vehicles are big robots. Many people believe all vehicles will be self-driving in the future. Driverless vehicle engineers will be responsible for designing these vehicles and making them work.

On the Job

Driverless vehicle engineers build robot cars that can think for themselves. The engineers design models on the computer. Then they run these models through **simulations** to test how the cars will work in real life. Once the engineers find something they think will work, they build a prototype. This prototype must be able to handle problems on the road in a split second without the aid of a driver. What if a person walks out in front of the robot car? The robot car must know to slam on the brakes. Engineers are still working on making driverless vehicle technology perfect.

Pay Range

Average salary = $240,000 per year.

Education and Skills

Driverless vehicle engineers have at least four years of college. They study mechanical engineering. They must know how cars and other machines work. They also study computer engineering. They have to program the car's brain. These engineers need to think creatively and solve problems. They must be able to work with others on a team.

FUN FACT

People have been talking about self-driving cars since the 1930s. But we are already using driverless trains. The first completely automated metro line was in Kobe, Japan. It was put into service in 1981.

The newest driverless cars do not have steering wheels, gas pedals, or brake pedals. They use large cameras to "see" the road.

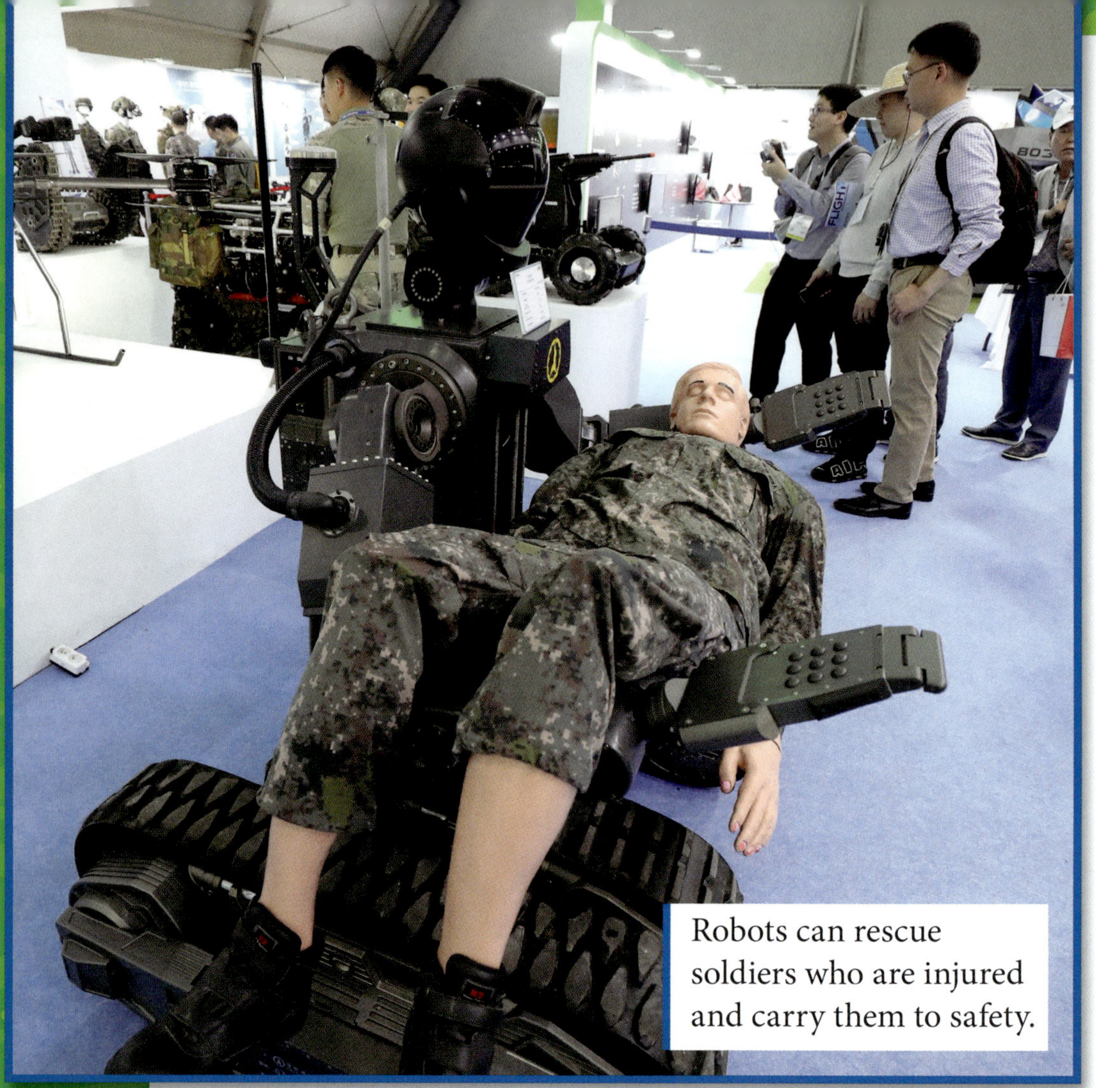

Robots can rescue soldiers who are injured and carry them to safety.

Military Worker

The military generally has the latest and greatest technology. They have the highest-flying planes. They drive the most advanced vehicles. And they use the fastest computers. They also have the most amazing robots. All of this advanced technology helps the military keep our country safe.

On the Job

The military uses robot technology in many ways. They use drones in the air. They use unmanned submarines in the sea. Soldiers roll robots into danger zones to defuse bombs and other explosives. Robots are also used to sneak into an area to find out where the enemy is. They are able to do things that human soldiers cannot safely do.

FUN FACT

The military is working on exoskeleton suits that are much like the Iron Man suits from the comics. These suits would give soldiers who wear them extra strength. They would even help soldiers run at fast speeds uphill.

Pay Range

Depends on terms of service and rank. Newly commissioned officers make about $40,000 per year.

Education and Skills

Most members of the military receive on-the-job training. The majority of military members go through basic training. This is a tough period of training. They have physical fitness sessions. They learn how to use weapons. They also are taught to follow orders from their leaders. After military service, many military members go on to college. Military members who work with robots might receive special training to continue getting the skills and knowledge they need.

Aerospace Scientist

People often think of robots when they picture outer space. Many science fiction books and movies feature robots. Those robots are fake. But there are lots of real ones that are helping humans learn more about flight and space travel.

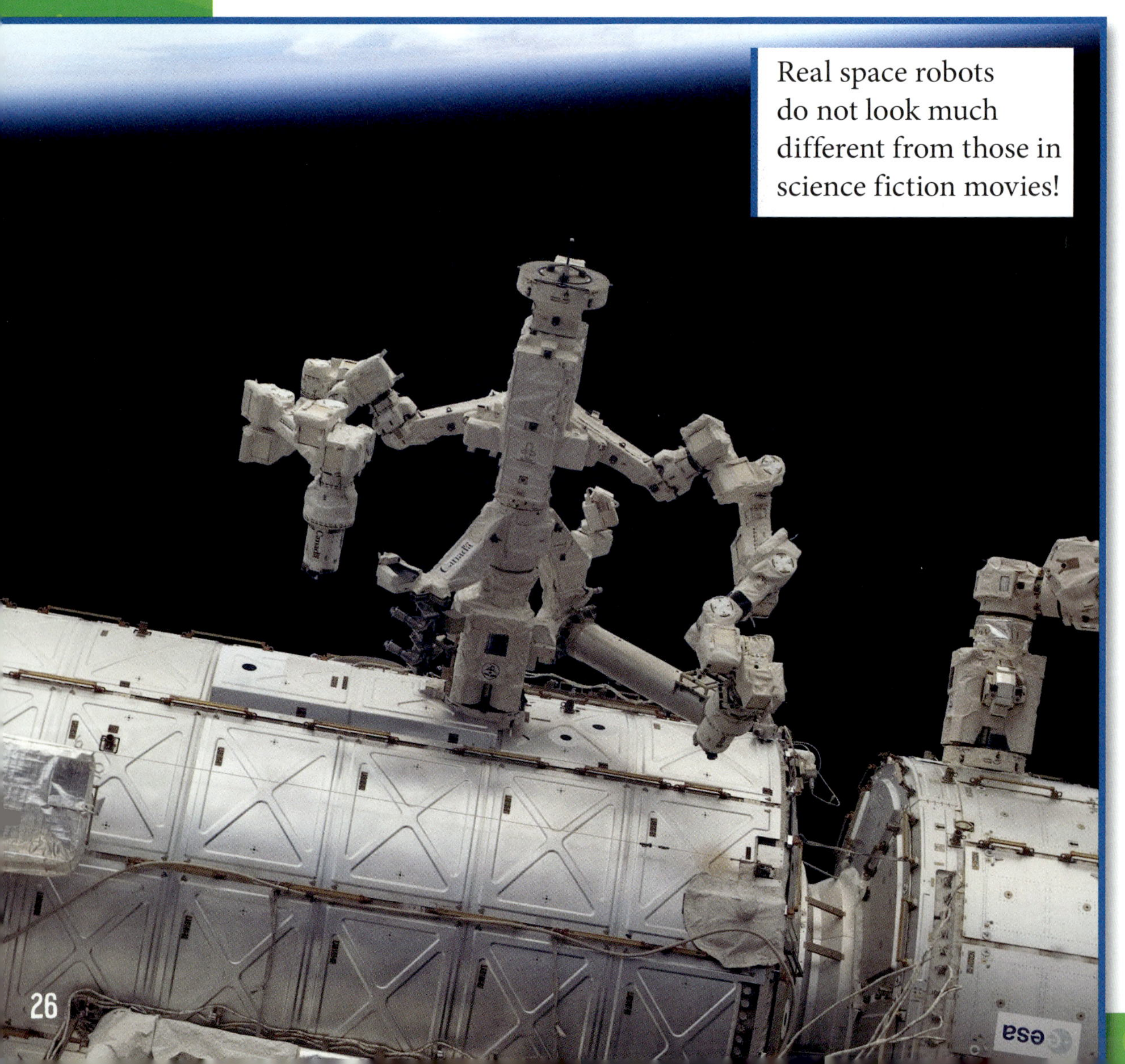

Real space robots do not look much different from those in science fiction movies!

On the Job

Robots take on many roles in the aerospace field. They help build space vehicles on Earth. They build planes and plane engines. Some robots even explore new horizons far from Earth. Robots are on the International Space Station (ISS). There are also robots on Mars called rovers. Aerospace scientists help design and build these robots. They also work alongside the robots. They perform important tasks with them.

FUN FACT

The Robonaut2 was the first human-like robot in space. It arrived on the International Space Station in 2011. It can crawl around on the outside of the space station and make repairs.

Pay Range

Average salary = $115,000 per year.

Education and Skills

Aerospace scientists have advanced college degrees. Many study chemistry, physics, and engineering. They are good at math and science. They are able to think outside the box. They must come up with creative solutions to problems. Some of these solutions might include building a robot to do a job.

Police use robots to patrol shopping centers and other public places.

Police Officer

Police officers make sure people obey the law. They help citizens stay safe. They protect people from those who might want to hurt them. Robots help police officers stay safe.

On the Job

Robots can be used by police officers in many ways. Police can fly drones over crowded areas. The drones take pictures and videos. They alert the police if they spot any unusual activities. In some places around the world, robots are members of the police force. They stand watch on city streets.

FUN FACT

Robocops can be programmed to talk in multiple languages. This allows the same type of robocop to be used in many countries around the world.

Pay Range

Average salary = $65,000 per year.

Education and Skills

Police officers are trained at police academies. They learn how to use weapons. They learn how to handle stressful situations. They must stay calm under pressure. They also have to pass several tests. The tests make sure they are physically fit and know the rules of being an officer. Police officers must be able to make good on-the-spot decisions. They must also be able to work well with others.

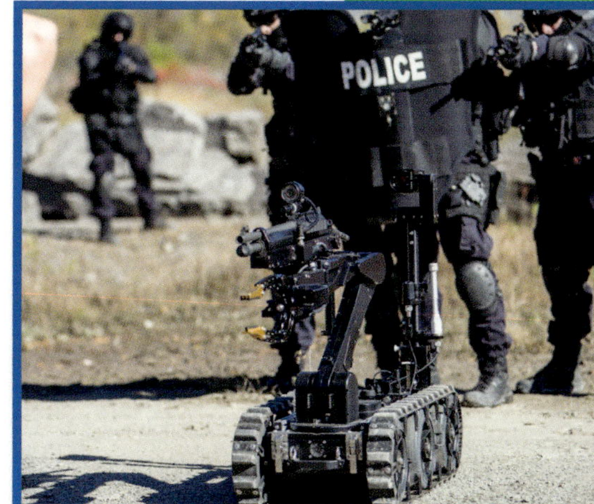

Robots can shield and protect police officers in dangerous situations.

Glossary

aerial (AYR-ee-uhl)—something that is done in the air

assembly line (uh-SEM-blee LYN)—a group of workers or machines that puts together a product

autonomous (aw-TAH-nuh-muhss)—able to control oneself; autonomous robots are not operated remotely by a person

commercial (kuh-MUHR-shuhl)—having to do with buying and selling things

digestive system (dye-JESS-tive SISS-tuhm)—the body organs that break down food into energy and get rid of waste

documentary (dahk-yuh-MEN-tuh-ree)—a movie or TV program about real situations and people

drone (DROHN)—an unmanned aircraft that is controlled from the ground

prototype (PROH-tuh-tipe)—the first version of an invention that tests an idea to see if it will work

script (SKRIPT)—the story for a play, movie, or television show

simulation (sim-yoo-LAY-shun)—a computer model of something in real life

urban (UR-bahn)—having to do with a city

Read More

Katovich, Bob. *Awesome Robotics Projects for Kids: 20 Original STEAM Robots and Circuits to Design and Build.* Emeryville, CA: Rockridge Press, 2019.

Schul, Christina. *Awesome Engineering Activities for Kids: 50+ Exciting STEAM Projects to Design and Build.* Emeryville, CA: Rockridge Press, 2019.

Smithbert, Angie, and Alexis Cornell. *Artificial Intelligence: Thinking Machines and Smart Robots with Science Activities for Kids.* White River Junction, VT: Nomad Press, 2018.

Swanson, Jennifer. *National Geographic Kids. Everything Robotics: All the Robotic Photos, Facts, and Fun!* Washington, D.C.: National Geographic, 2016.

Vordeman, Carol. *How to Be an Engineer.* New York: DK Publishing, 2018.

Internet Sites

Challenge: Robots!
https://nationalgeographic.org/interactive/challenge-robots/

Engineering for Kids: Robots
https://www.engineeringforkids.com/curriculum/robotics/

Robotics NASA
https://robotics.nasa.gov/edu/k-5.php

Index